God Speaks Through Suffering

God Speaks Through Suffering

T. B. Maston

WORD BOOKS, PUBLISHER · Waco, Texas

The Bible verse marked TLB is taken from *The Living Bible,
Paraphrased* (Wheaton: Tyndale House Publishers, 1971) and
used by permission. Quotations from the Today's English
Version of the Bible, copyright © American Bible Society
1976, are used by permission of the American Bible Society.

Quotations from the Revised Standard Version of
the Bible, copyrighted 1946, 1952, © 1971, 1973 by
the Division of Christian Education of the National
Council of the Churches of Christ in the U.S.A.
and used by permission.

ISBN 0–8499–2802–8
Library of Congress catalog card number: 77–76349
Printed in the United States of America

To
Tom Mc

Contents

Preface

Do you have some heavy burden to carry? Has some great sorrow come into your life? Are you personally suffering, or do you suffer because a member of your family or a friend suffers? If the answer is yes to any of these or to closely related questions, then this brief book has been written for you.

Like many of you, I have cried out, "Why suffering?" I have also struggled with the closely related question, What is God's relation to suffering?

Several years ago I felt I had to find a reasonably satisfactory answer to the preceding questions or lose my sanity and/or my faith. The position regarding suffering suggested in the following pages has been worked out, or possibly better, hammered out, because of my personal experience. The first chapter spells out briefly the major background for formulating that position. Most succeeding chapters will open with an actual case or experience which you will be challenged to think through.

The overall position and much of the content appeared in an earlier work, now out of print. This book is shorter and includes new and more specific chapter titles. The general structure and approach vary considerably from the former book.

As was true of the earlier book on suffering, the present one has been to an unusual degree a family production. My wife (Mommie) has contributed in many ways, directly and indirectly; many of her ideas have been incorporated. Eugene, our younger son, has shared in the problems and, I am sure, in the soul struggle that suffering brings. Tom Mc, our older son, has spent his life in a wheelchair. In a very real sense, this is his book. Without him it would never have been written.

Appreciation is expressed to friends who have consented for their experiences to be included and to be identified by name. Appreciation is also expressed to Mrs. Melvin Bridgford who again has prepared a manuscript of mine for publication.

T. B. M.

Unless otherwise indicated, all Scripture quotations are from the King James Version.

1.   Suffering:
A Personal Experience

Mommie and I have known many of the disappointments and have carried many of the burdens that come with life. For example, my dad, sister, and brother all died with cancer and experienced the intense suffering that cancer frequently brings. Our real struggle, however, with the problem of suffering began when our first child was born. I had stood by when he came into the world. When I got home, I sat down at the dining-room table and wept. It had been a trying, emotional experience. His mother had almost literally given her life that he might live. Why?

The question became louder and more persistent when we noticed that his development along some lines was slower than expected. Why? became a shout when we discovered that Tom Mc had been injured at birth. The inner struggle deepened as we took him to many doctors and several hospitals in search of help. We returned with saddened hearts as doctor after doctor told us: "We do not know anything that can be done for him. All you can do is take him home and give him the best possible care."

Much more is being done for the cerebral palsied today. When Tom Mc was a child, there were, as far as we could discover, only four doctors in the entire United States who seemingly gave any attention to cerebral palsy. We took him to two of those doctors—one in New York and the other in New Haven. Mommie, with the help of others, spent hours and hours for several years trying to help him talk and gain better control of his body.

Tom Mc is about as seriously handicapped physically as one can be. Almost every voluntary muscle of his body is affected. His mother or I have to do well-nigh everything for him. We dress and undress him, bathe him, clean his teeth, shave him daily, feed him, and even shift or turn him in bed. We usually have to get up two to a half-dozen times

[14]

each night. An unbroken night's sleep is a rarity. He cannot walk, talk, or even sit alone.

In spite of his handicap, we can usually communicate with Tom Mc. His *yes* is "I," which he can pronounce clearly. For *no*, he bats his eyelids. He also uses *I* when he wants something. We have lived with him long enough that we usually know what he wants. When we do not, we ask him, "Do you want . . . ?" When we hit the right thing, his *I* tells us. You can imagine, however, our frustration when he wants something, when something is really wrong, or when he hurts somewhere and we are unable to find out what or where it is.

Fortunately for him, and for us, Tom Mc has unusually good health—better than any member of the family. His mother and I would much rather be sick than for him to be sick. Just imagine, for example, how it would be to have a severe head cold and be unable to clear your throat or blow your nose. He can do neither.

I have not shared the preceding to appeal to your sympathy but so you will know that what I say in the following pages is not mere theory. We have sat where many of you sit. We have walked and are still walking the road that many of you are on at the present time.

As some of you know from personal experience, our Tom Mc has not been exclusively a problem or a burden. It may be unfair to speak of him as a burden at all. There are things about him that add joy to our lives. He has a good mind and evidently gets considerable satisfaction out of life. Naturally, his mind has not developed normally. How could it when he cannot turn pages to read and cannot ask questions?

He has his favorite television programs and enjoys good music and an occasional dramatic production. He goes to church with us regularly and is loved by and responds readily to many of our fellow church members. He loves the outdoors and likes to sit in the yard in his wheelchair and "watch the world go by." Our home is on a corner lot, and he prefers to sit where he can watch both streets and the school playground across from our house.

He is timid around strangers, particularly around those who are ill at ease in his presence. He is fond of children, particularly those not afraid of his wheelchair. He usually has a captivating smile and a twinkle in his eyes for those, regardless of age, who reach out in love to him and establish good rapport with him.

He is a good traveler and has shared with his mother and daddy and his younger brother trips to many parts of the United States. The other members of the family had been on overseas trips. Tom Mc had not until a few years ago. An invitation came for me to teach in Beirut, Lebanon. I would not go and leave Mommie to care for Tom Mc by herself as long as I would have to be away. When I mentioned the invitation to her, she said, "I am game. I am willing for us to see how Tom Mc will travel by air."

He had never been on a plane until we flew to New York. We spent a few days with his younger brother, who lives in New York City. We then flew to Beirut, with stops at Paris and Rome. We had arranged our schedule so we would not have to change planes; so we were en route fourteen hours. Tom Mc made the journey like a seasoned traveler. On the return trip we toured the Holy Land, spent some time in Rome and Zurich, and then toured Great Britain by car.

Since then, Mommie, Tom Mc, and I have made extensive trips to South America and Hawaii. Tom Mc's wheelchair goes wherever he goes. Our travel has meant a great deal to him, and he has blessed the lives of many. A missionary friend on a field we visited was kind enough to say that Mommie and I had been a blessing to many, but he added that Tom Mc's presence had been the greatest blessing.

Through the years we have felt that it was best to keep Tom Mc in our home. It is not necessary to spell out why we made this decision. We are not critical of others who have placed a handicapped son or daughter in a special school or institution. This decision must be personal and can be soul-searching.

As you would know, Tom Mc's presence in our home has influenced in many ways the other members of the family. For example, his presence has limited to some degree my activities and movements. It does seem, however, that God has compensated for any activities I have given up. For example, the fact that I have stayed closer at home, particularly on weekends, than I might have otherwise, has made it possible for me to have a more extensive writing ministry.

This is enough of our personal experience. As we proceed with our study, may our heavenly Father help you to work through to a personally satisfying answer to the perplexing companion questions: Why suffering and What is God's relation to human suffering? May the position to which you come strengthen your faith in God and in his goodness and grace. May you hear him speak to you in and through your suffering.

2. Suffering:

Its Prevalence

What is the nature of your sorrow or suffering? Have you recently lost a loved one? Has some tragedy come into your life? Do you carry a burden that time cannot heal or lighten? Do you have a son or a daughter with some serious physical or mental handicap? Are you personally suffering with arthritis or some incurable disease?

Whatever your sorrow or the cause of your suffering, if you look carefully, you will discover: (1) that suffering and sorrow of some kind and to some degree are the common lot of humankind, (2) that some carry heavier burdens and walk in deeper shadows than you, and (3) that many people have the same type of suffering as you or carry burdens similar to yours. For example, in our household we scarcely knew there was such a thing as cerebral palsy until Tom Mc came. Since then, we have seen the cerebral palsied almost everywhere we go. You may have had only a vague idea about mongolism until your mongoloid son or daughter was born. Now you recognize the distinctive marks of the mongoloid wherever you see them.

UNIVERSALITY OF SUFFERING

We can sum up by simply saying that suffering and the shadows that suffering brings come to all: the young and the old, the wise and the unwise, the educated and the uneducated, the good and the bad, to those of all classes and colors. Life has not played a trick on you or me when suffering comes. We have simply joined the human race. Longfellow said:

> Into each life some rain must fall,
> Some days must be dark and dreary.

Christians should remember that this will be true of believers as well as unbelievers. God does not build a protective wall around his children, refusing to let any harm come to them. He has not promised to protect them in some miraculous way from suffering. If the children of God were shielded in some unusual way, we would live in an unpredictable world. We could not depend on the laws of life.

How grateful we should be, however, that our heavenly Father will not permit sorrow, suffering, or burdens of any kind to separate us from him and his love. If there is any separation, it will be our responsibility. Really, at times it seems that the darker the shadows, the clearer and brighter his presence.

Spelling out the various kinds or causes of suffering graphically points up its prevalence. As you consider various types of suffering, you may find that several apply to you personally. Think, however, not so much of yourself as of family, neighbors, friends, and fellow church members.

Sooner or later, sorrow comes to all because of the death of a loved one. It may be a young child deprived of a father's or a mother's love and care. Or, it may be a teenager who loses mother or father when he or she needs them most. Sorrow comes to mature children in the loss of an aging parent, and there is the deep anguish that comes when a husband or wife dies. This sense of loss can be very acute whether the couple has lived together for a short or a long time. Some of the loneliest people in the world are older people who have lost a companion after many years. They can understand what my mother said some years after dad's death: "No one knows how lonely it has been since dad went away."

Gaines S. Dobbins and his wife had been married for approximately sixty-two years when she passed away. He, a well-known lecturer, writer, and long-time theological professor, wrote in a beautiful way concerning his wife's death.

She had been in a nursing home for the last six years of her life. Concerning those years, he said, "My companion's journey led to the end which we call death but to which she looked forward as release from inescapable infirmity."

About his visits to the nursing home, he wrote: "And so for six years, as the day ended and the shadows gathered, I stood beside my Beloved's bed in the nursing home, and said, 'I must go now before Old Man Dark catches me. Good-night, I'll see you in the morning.' Then one day the darkness we call Death gathered. The light in her life grew dim and went out. I kissed her cold and voiceless lips and said: 'Good-night, I'll see you in the morning.' "

What a triumphant note!

Incidentally, if you want to see suffering of all kinds, mental and emotional as well as physical, visit a nursing home. Some in those homes are well adjusted and reasonably happy, but many are not. Some are ambulatory; others are in wheelchairs; and still others are confined to their beds. Some are extremely lonely, largely neglected and forgotten by family and friends. Many are simply waiting for death, which will be a relief to them.

PHYSICAL SUFFERING

The many causes of physical suffering include heart trouble, strokes, asthma, cancer, multiple sclerosis, muscular dystrophy, and cystic fibrosis, among others. Some of these, at the present level of medical knowledge, have to be considered creeping death. Loved ones have to stand by helplessly and see the victims worsen gradually until death comes.

The list of the different types of physical suffering would not be complete without mentioning children who are born crippled. Some are born with twisted, deformed bodies, while others come into the world without one or more limbs. In addition, blindness and deafness are often congenital.

Accidents are another cause of untold physical suffering for many. In addition to the large number of accidental deaths each year, many victims of accidents, as some of you know, are crippled for life.

MENTAL SUFFERING

In addition to the suffering that comes because of death or disease, a great deal of suffering results from mental illness and emotional disturbance of various kinds. In the United States there are approximately as many hospital beds occupied by the mentally ill as by the physically ill. The mentally and emotionally disturbed who are not hospitalized may suffer more personally than those who have been institutionalized.

Then there are the mentally retarded. It is difficult to know how much they suffer personally. Most of those who are surrounded with an atmosphere of love and understanding seem to be happy. Unfortunately, some are rejected by members of their families and by neighbors. They must suffer a great deal. Just the fact that they sense they are different undoubtedly causes considerable suffering to some.

Much suffering of the mentally and emotionally disturbed stems from the attitude of people toward them. A woman I have known for many years has spent some time in the past in a hospital for the mentally disturbed. In recent conversations with her and her husband she made a couple of statements that have bothered me. One of the statements was: "When I was having my problems, I found more understanding from my non-Christian friends than from my fellow church members." The other statement, equally disturbing and challenging, was: "I don't think the folks want me up there." "Up there" referred to her church.

I assured her that the latter was not true of all her fellow church members. I was sure, however, that it was true of some. How can we explain the attitude that many Christians have toward the mentally ill, the emotionally disturbed? Christians should seek, in this as well as in other areas, to have more of the spirit and mind of Christ. He understood and reached out in love to help the mentally ill as well as the physically sick and handicapped.

There are many other causes of suffering. In some homes, there is constant tension. Although these homes may have held together, the husband and wife have failed to make a satisfactory adjustment to each other. Other homes have been broken by separation and/or divorce. Millions suffer the result of alcoholism, drug addiction, gambling and crime. Some parents suffer because of disappointment in a son or daughter. This disappointment may come to the best of Christian homes.

SUFFERING WITH OTHERS

There is a type of suffering that has been mentioned but possibly should be underscored. It is, in a sense, vicarious and is involved to some degree in almost every case of suffering. It is that which relatives or friends experience when a loved one suffers, and it becomes most severe when they can do nothing to relieve the suffering.

Parents of retarded children are among those who suffer "with others." They may suffer personally and directly, but their deepest concern is for the welfare and security of the son or daughter. This is also frequently true of parents of the physically handicapped. While the handicapped son or daughter may be a major care to parents, it is possible that they suffer *with* him or her more than *because* of him or her. Every time he or she tries and cannot do things that normal children do, there is a deep hurt within them.

One source of suffering for parents of a seriously handicapped or retarded child may be their struggle of soul about what to do with him. Should the child be kept in the home or institutionalized? Evelyn Phillips knows by personal experience the soul struggle of such a decision. Her husband and the father of her only child, a mongoloid son, died suddenly when Mark was ten years of age. Mrs. Phillips faced many decisions and problems at that time, but "one problem was devastating—the proper care and training for Mark." This became for her "an agonizing problem for the next six years."

Although she increasingly realized that she could not provide in the home all that Mark needed, she could not bring herself to send him to an institution. She felt she could do a better job than any institution. Furthermore, she believed it was her place to care for her own. However, she realized more and more that there were some things she could not give him or do for him. In the meantime, she discovered a five-hundred-acre ranch operated for retarded young men. It was well equipped and staffed with personnel trained in special education. She says, "I began to feel that the best thing I could give my boy would be the opportunity to get close to nature and learn to do some job well."

After Mark's two years on the farm, his mother still has some struggle of soul. Her conclusion, however, is, "I feel that I have done the right thing," the thing that is best for Mark. She thanks God for "strength to endure," "for friends and family who have helped," and for a place like the farm for Mark.

If you ("you" in this paragraph refers to father and/or mother) are struggling with a decision similar to Evelyn Phillips's, permit me to suggest several guidelines: (1) No one can tell you what you ought to do with your child. There is no general rule that will cover every case. (2) If you are convinced that it will be best for your child to be sent to a school or an institution, you should be willing to send him. (3) On the other hand, if you believe it will be best for your handicapped son or daughter to stay at home, you should be willing to adjust to whatever inconvenience and limitations this will create. (4) Naturally, in making the decision you should carefully consider the effect on other children in the home and on the family as a unit. (5) Ask the Lord to give you wisdom to know what you ought to do and, once knowing, the courage to do it.

You know, of course, that such a decision is potentially very important for the son or daughter, for other children in the home, for you and your companion, and for relatives and friends.

Almost every type of sorrow and suffering is evident in our church and community. We have been members of our church for many years. Many of the members have been or are neighbors and close friends of ours. Our church includes some of the best people we have ever known. Some of those people have carried unusually heavy burdens. Mommie and I sit behind the back pew with Tom Mc in his wheelchair between us. As I have frequently looked over the congregation and have seen the many who suffer for one reason or another, my heart has cried out with the prophet, "Comfort ye, comfort ye my people, saith your God" (Isa. 40:1).

Regardless of the reason for your suffering or sorrow, I hope that you will find, as you read these pages, some encouragement, some ray of hope, some word from our heavenly Father.

3.   The Laws of Life and Suffering

Jack was a member of my Sunday school class, a neighbor, and a friend. He had a relatively severe heart condition. His doctor had warned him that he should avoid undue excitement and strenuous exercise. One day on his way home from work, Jack saw some neighbor boys playing touch football. He entered into the game with his usual vigor and enthusiasm. Approximately ten minutes after he arrived at home, he had a heart attack. Before an ambulance could get him to the hospital, he was dead.

A young man, caught up in a fanatical religious

movement, jumped from a second-floor balcony to the ground below. He had insisted, "God will take care of me." Both his ankles were broken.

Who or what was responsible for Jack's death and the young man's broken ankles? In what sense and to what degree was God responsible?

The questions, Why suffering? and In what way and to what degree is God responsible for suffering? disturb the mind and challenge the faith of many who suffer and those who stand by and suffer with them.

Some people contend that suffering comes without "rhyme or reason." They claim there is no cause-and-effect relationship in the area of sorrow and suffering. This position is out of harmony with the kind of world in which we live. It is not satisfying from the strictly intellectual viewpoint, and certainly it does not satisfy the child of God.

MEANING OF "LAWS OF LIFE"

We will be helped in our search for answers if we understand the nature of the laws of life. One definition of *law* is "a sequence of events in nature or in human activity that has been observed to occur with unvarying uniformity under the same conditions." *Law* can also mean "any rule or principle expected to be observed: as, the laws of health" (*Webster's New World Dictionary*). These definitions describe what I prefer to call the "basic laws of life." They are laws that cannot be broken; they break the one who breaks them.

The young man who jumped from the balcony and broke his ankles evidently violated a basic law of life, the law of gravity. It also seems clear that my friend Jack broke a basic health law.

The operation of the basic laws of life is clearly seen in the natural order. It does not take a scientist or the son of a scientist to know that we live in a universe of law. There is regularity or dependability in the universe. As certainly as the sun goes down at night, it will come up in the morning. The seasons follow one another in regular order.

My personal conviction is that all of life is governed by basic laws written into the nature of human beings and their world. This conception is foundational in my theology, or philosophy, of suffering. In other words, most, if not all, suffering results from the operation of certain fundamental laws. Some of these laws may be incorporated in the statutes of states or nations. Whether or not this is true will not affect their validity or their operation.

The operation of the universe in harmony with

laws written into its nature gives us a dependable, stable universe. When everything in the world created by humankind is changing, things created by God are dependable.

We may not and do not know all of the laws of life. We may see the "effect" and yet not know the "cause." This is true of some of the most serious illnesses. Scientists and others are on a constant search for the causes of such illnesses and for other basic laws, but, known or unknown, the laws continue to operate.

HEALTH LAWS

Unfortunately, some ministers and other Christian leaders tend to attribute everything that happens to the direct, miraculous intervention of God. For example, a family may violate every known health law. As a result, illness and ultimately death may come to a member of the family. At the funeral the following statement by Job may be quoted: "The Lord gave, and the Lord hath taken away; blessed be the name of the Lord" (Job 1:21). But did the Lord take away? If so, how? Did God step in in some direct way to take the life, or did he simply permit death to come?

Some who attribute all suffering to the direct action of God rebel against him. They should recognize that in many and possibly most cases of serious illness or suffering God would have had to intervene in some miraculous way to have prevented it. This would have been true of our Tom Mc. He was injured because a doctor made a mistake. A young man dived into water that was too shallow, broke his neck, and now he is paralyzed from his shoulders down. Why should or can we or he blame God?

Although the laws of mental health are not as generally or as widely known as the laws of physical health and are seemingly more complex, they evidently operate in much the same way. If they are observed, mental health follows. If ignored or violated, mental or emotional illness comes. For example, one thing that is definitely detrimental to mental health and emotional stability is too much preoccupation with oneself. In other words, one of the healthiest things we can do is to become so concerned about others and so active in serving them in the name of the Lord that we largely forget ourselves. To adapt a statement by Jesus, we evidently find mental health as well as life on its highest level by denying or forgetting self (see Matt. 16:25).

Some mental attitudes such as jealousy and hate quite evidently violate the laws of mental health. For example, when one is jealous of another, he hurts himself much more than he hurts the one of whom he is jealous. The same is true of hate. When one hates another, the person he hurts the most is himself. One cannot violate the laws of wholesome personality without paying the price in one's own personality.

RELATION TO OTHER LAWS

How are the "laws of life" related to civil or criminal laws and to the laws and commandments of God as recorded in the Scriptures?

In at least two ways the basic laws of life differ from civil and/or criminal laws. (1) The latter may be violated and one may not be caught or punished. For example, one may have violated every traffic regulation of the city or community and never have received a ticket or paid a fine. This is in marked contrast to the basic laws that are written into our nature and the nature of the world. The penalty for the "laws of life" is inescapable. (2) The penalty for the violation of civil or criminal law is assessed by judge or jury. The penalty for the violation of the basic laws of life is inherent in the laws themselves. The penalty may be delayed in coming, but sooner or later it will come. Paul's statement "Whatsoever a man soweth, that shall he also reap" (Gal. 6:7) applies to the operation of the fundamental laws of life.

In contrast to their relation to civil and criminal laws, the basic laws of life are closely related to, if not identifiable with, the fundamental laws or commandments and principles found in the Scriptures. This is true of the fundamental moral laws of the Old Testament which express and conform to the basic laws God has written into our nature. You remember that Jesus said, "The sabbath was made for man, and not man for the sabbath" (Mark 2:27). What Jesus said concerning the sabbath could be said for many other laws found in the Old Testament, including the Ten Commandments. They were provided for a person's good, and there is a sense in which they are written into our natures. This means, among other things, that these commandments should not be grievous or burdensome to us (1 John 5:3, RSV). We should seek to know them and to obey them.

The basic laws of life also closely relate to and express the teachings of the New Testament. Think of how the Golden Rule (Matt. 7:12) would apply to many human situations. Then there are the teachings of Jesus on love which he makes broad enough and deep enough to include one's enemies as well as one's neighbors or friends (Matt. 5:43–47). In other words, the teachings of the New Testament in general and of Jesus in particular express and conform to the basic laws as God has written them into our nature and into the nature of our world.

It is possible that some laws of life may be set aside or abrogated at times. When this is done, it will usually be in harmony with a higher law. Setting aside a basic law may be achieved in some areas in the natural order through the ingenuity of man. For example, every time a jet plane takes off from a runway, it violates or sets aside the law of gravity. To achieve this purpose certain other laws have been discovered and are utilized.

In addition to what man can do, it is possible, as we shall discuss more fully later, that God steps into the picture at times and sets aside some law. We can be sure that any time he does this it will be in harmony with a higher law.

The fact that basic laws of life at times may be set aside or abrogated does not nullify the fact that we live in a universe of law. Neither does it nullify the idea that the penalty for violating the basic laws of life is inherent in the laws themselves.

The consequences, good or bad, pleasant or painful, are a natural result of keeping or breaking the laws of life. This is true, not only in our personal lives, but in human relations in general: in the home, the shop, the office, the legislative hall—wherever men are thrown with one another. Basic laws govern the relation of races, nations, and cultures. Harmonious relations in all these areas result from obedience to those laws.

4. Sin and Suffering

A friend and fellow church member died a short time ago with emphysema and heart complications that frequently accompany serious cases of emphysema. Toward the last it was extremely difficult for him to walk across the room or even to carry on a conversation. He was constantly gasping for breath. A tank of oxygen was kept close by at all times.

He said on more than one occasion, "I smoked too many cigarettes for too many years."

Do you see how his illness and death relate to the discussion in chapter 3? What has medical science revealed in recent years concerning the relation of smoking, not only to emphysema, but to lung cancer and other serious illnesses? Had my friend sinned by smoking? How would you defend your answer?

MEANING OF SIN

Whether my friend had sinned or not will be determined to a large degree by the meaning of *sin*. If *sin* is restricted to the violation of some formalized or verbalized law or commandment, then he had not sinned. Also, we could conclude that most suffering is not the result of sin. But if it is a sin to violate or live out of harmony with the basic laws of life which may or may not have been verbalized, then he had sinned.

My viewpoint is that *sin* is a violation of any law of God. Furthermore, we have suggested that the basic laws of life are from God. If this broader view of sin is accepted, then it is clear that most, if not all, suffering is the result of sin. This perspective is in harmony with the idea, prevalent in the Scriptures, of sin as a transgression or a straying out of the way that God has marked out. The basic laws of life set limits within which God expects us to live, and they harmonize with the nature he has given us. To stray from them is to violate God's purposes for us, and hence it is sin.

When we conclude that there is a close relation between sin and·most, if not all, suffering, there are still some important unanswered questions. One of the most important is: If sin is the cause of suffering, whose sin is it—the sin of the sufferer or of someone else? This question has challenged men and women through the centuries.

The preceding question evidently concerned the disciples of our Lord. When they saw a man blind from his birth, they asked Jesus, "Master, who did sin, this man, or his parents, that he was born blind" (John 9:2). They seemingly thought his blindness a direct result of sin, and they were not thinking of sin in general. His blindness, so they reasoned, was punishment sent upon him or his parents for his sin or theirs. Today's English Version translates the verse as follows: "Teacher, whose sin was it that caused him to be born blind? His own or his parents' sin?" The disciples expressed the orthodox Jewish perspective: suffering was sent as punishment for personal sin. One was the cause, and the other, the effect.

Jesus did not agree with this position. His word to the disciples was, "Neither hath this man sinned, nor his parents (John 9:3), or, as Today's English Version says, "His blindness has nothing to do with his sins or his parents' sins." Then Jesus revealed that the man's blindness would be used "to demonstrate the power of God" (John 9:3, TLB).

Jesus did not mean that the man or his parents had not sinned although certainly the man could not have sinned before he was born. Jesus simply said that his blindness was not sent by God as punishment for sin.

WHOSE SIN

We should not conclude from Jesus' reply that he did not think there was any relationship between sin and suffering. We do not know what his reply would have been if the disciples had asked, "Is sin the cause of this man's blindness?" or, "Who sinned that this man was born blind?" We do know that when Jesus saw the man in the temple who had been healed beside the pool of Bethesda, he said to him, "Behold, thou art made whole: sin no more, lest a worst thing come unto thee" (John 5:14; cf. Matt. 9:2). This at least implies a possible direct relation between personal sin and some suffering.

But can someone other than the sufferer be the cause of his suffering? If so, we may conclude that much and possibly most suffering results from someone's sin other than the sufferer.

Thomas Carlyle once said, "Sin is, has been, and ever will be the parent of misery." I would agree with Carlyle if he meant sin in general and misery in general. I would disagree if he meant the sin and misery of a particular individual.

To keep ourselves from feeling too smug and selfsatisfied, we should admit that we have "sinned, and come short of the glory of God" (Rom. 3:23), that among us "there is none righteous, no, not one" (v. 10), and that "all we like sheep have gone astray; we have turned every one to his own way" (Isa. 53:6). We should confess, Christians and non-Christians, that we have sinned against God and his purposes to the degree that we would deserve as punishment the sorrow and suffering that come into our lives.

Furthermore, we should recognize that some suffering may come as a result of our personal sin. If the punishment for violating the basic laws of life is inherent in the laws, then we can be sure that any time we violate those laws we will sooner or later suffer the consequences. Let us repeat, however, that the suffering in such cases is not sent in some miraculous way by the Lord; rather, he permits the basic laws to operate. This was the case with my friend who suffered and ultimately died with emphysema. God did not send the suffering and the death. Certain health laws had been violated. The disease was the result.

SUFFERING OF THE INNOCENT

One thing that keeps man searching for an answer concerning the relation of sin and suffering is the suffering of the innocent. Would God cause a son to be born crippled or a daughter a mongoloid to punish the sins of a father or mother? Since the baby could not sin before birth, that would be sending suffering on the innocent to punish the guilty. Everything we know about the God revealed by Jesus suggests he would not do that.

Then what about the innocent bystander who is seriously wounded during a shoot-out between police and a holdup man? What about one who is crippled for life when struck by a car driven by a drunk? Much suffering is not the result of the sin or sins of the sufferer.

God may, and evidently does, frequently use suffering, not sent directly by him, as a means to chasten his children. We should remember, however, that the main purpose of his chastening is to purify and mature rather than to punish. If we will let him, our all-wise and loving heavenly Father will use for our good any suffering that comes to us regardless of why it comes. He will speak to us through our suffering. What we let God do to us and for us through suffering is much more important than for us to understand fully why the suffering comes.

SUMMARY

Let us summarize what we have suggested concerning the relation of sin and suffering.

1. Sin is the violation of any law or purpose of God—written or unwritten. This includes the basic laws of life that are written into our nature.

2. When this broader perspective concerning sin is accepted, it means that there is a direct relation between sin and most if not all suffering. If there was no sin in the world there would be little if any suffering.

3. Suffering comes in the vast majority of cases because some basic law has been ignored or violated.

4. If suffering is punishment, the punishment comes largely through the operation of the basic laws of life. As we have previously stated, the penalty for the violation of those laws is inherent in the laws. This means that it is inevitable.

[45]

5. Some suffering results from the personal sin of the sufferer.

6. There are many occasions, however, when there is no evident direct relationship between the sin of the sufferer and his suffering. His suffering may come because others have sinned or even because a community or one or more of its institutions or agencies have sinned, such as the home, the school, the church.

7. The preceding means that we may not only reap what we sow, we may also reap what others sow. We should also remember that others may reap what we sow.

5. The Will of God and Suffering

I first knew Marie Miller as a dedi-
cated, dynamic Christian leader on a
university campus. Later she was a student of mine
in the theological seminary where I taught. She was
an outstanding student with excellent prospects for
a life of service to God and to her fellowman. Near
the close of her training she began to have trouble
with her eyes and some other minor health problems. After a considerable period of time, multiple
sclerosis was diagnosed.

She offered to release the young man, George
Threlkeld, to whom she was engaged. George re-

fused. They married. Recently, after more than twenty years of progressive death, she passed away. For many of those years George or someone else had to do practically everything for her. Personal suffering was considerably increased for Marie because she retained an alert mind until the end.

Was Marie's suffering in harmony with or expressive of the will of God? What about the suffering of George and of other loved ones as they watched her lose more and more control of her body? Was their suffering within the will of God?

WILL OF GOD AND FREEDOM OF MAN

Because God is sovereign, he must be related in some way to suffering. Is he directly or indirectly responsible? Does he send it, or does he simply permit it? In what way and to what degree is suffering within his will?

It can be quite important for one who suffers to answer the preceding questions. His or her answers may determine to a considerable degree his or her reaction to suffering and attitude toward the Lord. George and Marie evidently found the right answers. Otherwise, they could not have continued through the years to live fruitful, victorious Christian lives.

A mistaken conception concerning God's relation to suffering affects adversely the attitude of some people, even active Christians, toward God when suffering and/or sorrow comes into their lives. Some turn away from God. Others fatalistically accept the suffering and resign themselves to what they interpret to be the will of God. This attitude or reaction frequently means a dreary, defeated life.

A wrong interpretation of God's relation to suffering may stem from a misunderstanding concerning the sovereignty of God. Many Christians are fatalists. When tragedy strikes or suffering comes, they say, "I guess it is the will of God; I will have to accept it."

A fine line distinguishes between the sovereignty of God and fatalism. One can believe strongly in the former, which is clearly taught in Scriptures, and still not be a fatalist. After all, God created human beings with freedom of will. In other words, a person can and does decide, to a considerable degree, what happens to him or her. An individual has enough freedom to be responsible for himself or herself and before God.

Our finite minds may not be able to understand how God's sovereignty and an individual's freedom can be made compatible, but both are found in Scriptures. Our God who is infinite can do some things we cannot do and cannot even comprehend. He can give us freedom and still retain his sovereignty.

The freedom that God gives includes freedom either to obey or to disobey his laws. Also, God gives us freedom to search for and to discover laws that are not now known. We seem to have an innate desire to seek the ways of God in the world. This is our chief hope for the ultimate conquest of some of the unknown causes of suffering and sorrow.

DISTINCTIONS WITHIN THE WILL OF GOD

Another factor in misunderstanding God's relation to human suffering is an inadequate view or mistaken conception concerning the will of God. His will is so broad, so deep, and so complex that it is difficult for us to understand it. The problem is that we tend to attribute everything that happens to the will of God. Unless we make some distinctions regarding or within the will of God, we tend to become fatalistic. That is one reason people frequently say, "It would not have happened unless it was the will of God." In other words, they believe that everything is included in or is expressive of his will.

Leslie Weatherhead has made a threefold distinction among what he calls the ultimate will of God, the intentional will of God, and the circumstantial will of God. God's ultimate will is his big, overall redemptive purpose. No person, combination of persons, nation, or combination of nations can defeat that will. In God's ultimate will his sovereignty is fully expressed. The other two, the intentional will and the circumstantial will of God, are closely related if not identical to what others have called God's perfect or directive will and his permissive will.

If we make use of these distinctions, we can correctly conclude that most suffering is an expression of God's circumstantial or permissive will. It is not the result of the operation of his intentional, perfect, or directive will. If God could have his way and at the same time leave men and women free, it seems clear that he would prefer for there to be no sorrow or suffering. I believe this is true because of the attitude of Jesus toward the suffering of people while he walked among them. He used his power to relieve suffering rather than to send it. I also believe this is God's attitude toward suffering because there will be a place and time when "God shall wipe away all tears" from the eyes of his redeemed ones, "and there shall be no more death, neither sorrow, nor crying, neither shall there be any more pain: for the former things are passed away" (Rev. 21:4).

So when we hear someone say, "All suffering is the will of God," we should ask, "What do you mean by the 'will of God'?" If one means God's permissive, circumstantial will, then I agree. If one means God's perfect or intentional will, then I would have to disagree. Most suffering is God's will only in the sense that he permits it to come. Notice the use again of the word *most*. *Most* has to be used, not only because of the suffering that comes as a result of natural catastrophes that we do not understand, but also I do not believe any person has the wisdom or the right to say how God will always operate.

Now, what do you say concerning Marie's condition? How were her problem and the suffering and sorrow that it brought to her, to George, and to loved ones related to or expressive of the will of God? I think you know my answer. Do you agree?

If we understand that most suffering is simply permitted by God, will you not agree that we will no longer tend to blame the Lord for our suffering? Our main question will not be, Who did sin? or, Why suffering? but, What will God do for me and for others in and through my suffering?

The Will of God and the Laws of Life

Life is governed by basic laws. God is our Creator and also Creator of the laws that he has written into our nature and into the nature of the world.

These basic laws, being in harmony with our nature, are for our good. It is common sense to seek to know and to live in accord with these laws. However, since God has created us with freedom of will, we are free to obey or disobey those laws. We should never forget, however, that the consequences of obedience or disobedience will sooner or later inevitably follow. It possibly should be added that the latter will be true unless someone—God or a person—intervenes. It should also be said again that the disobedience that results in suffering may be by someone other than the sufferer.

God, who is a God of order, sees fit, with rare exceptions, to let the basic laws of life operate. In other words, there is a cause, known or unknown, for every effect. For example, in the case of Marie, we may not know much about the cause of multiple sclerosis, but we can be sure there is a cause. Also, so far we may not know a cure, but when it is discovered, it will be in harmony with or expressive of some of the basic laws of life.

[53]

Let me relate another incident. I can still visualize where the young man sat in a class of mine. He and his wife were preparing for overseas missionary service. She was a nurse and worked in one of the hospitals in our city. At the end of the day she came by, picked up her husband, and they drove to a small town relatively close by where he served as pastor.

One afternoon on the way home their car was struck by a freight train, and both were killed instantly. No one could understand the reason for the accident. It was a clear day, and there was a good view of the railroad track in both directions.

Was it God's will that Bill and his wife were killed? How far and in what way was God responsible for their deaths? Will you agree that he did not take their lives? A basic law applied to the situation. God did not see fit to set it aside, and the result was inevitable.

A searching question for some of us may be, Should we expect God in some miraculous way to shield or protect us from suffering and sorrow? Should Mommie and I have expected our heavenly Father to protect or shield us from the results of a mistake when Tom Mc was born? That has not been an easy question for us to ask and answer.

Closely akin to the preceding question is another: Should we expect protection or relief from the operation of the laws of life that would not be available to others? In other words, should we ask God to keep us or relieve us from sorrow and suffering unless we pray the same prayer for others? Do you agree that it is hard for us not to become selfish in praying for protection or for relief from suffering?

If you are disturbed by some of the preceding statements and questions, I hope your disturbance will be only temporary. I trust that as you seek to think through these things the ultimate result will be a clarification of your thinking and the strengthening of your faith in the goodness of our God.

6.   The Miracles of God
and Suffering

Clifton E. Harris, a doctor friend
of mine, had an unusual experience.
Following a near-fatal automobile accident and
subsequent arthritis, he had been confined to a
wheelchair. His suffering was severe. He attended
a religious service that included an emphasis on
healing. Toward the climax of the service he stood
up, left his wheelchair, and removed his full-length
leather leg brace. He tested his leg and found that
the pain had eased. He could "jog" and walk with
a strength he had not felt for twenty years. After a
few moments on the platform, he walked out and

drove home. He still has a noticeable limp, but the pain has not returned.

You may be interested to know that Dr. Harris says, "Because of my complete discipline as a doctor, I have never mentioned relative to myself the word *heal*." He adds, "I can truly say that for two years I have not needed the wheelchair and have had no pain. I have not missed one hour from my long work day due to any illness or disability."

Dr. Harris further asserts, "No one understands or can define satisfactorily to me what healing is: when it begins or when it ends. Any sort of thinking doctor must accept this without question!"

Several years ago, before the days of the so-called miracle drugs, I had the worst type of pneumonia. I went as close to death as one can go and come back to live. Doctors, nurses, and friends did not think I could survive. I may have been delirious at the time, but I still remember clearly two occasions when it seemed that God gave me a chance to choose to live or die. I told him it was perfectly all right with me to die—I was not afraid of death. But I did say that for the sake of my family, Mommie and our two boys, and for the sake of my work which I felt was incomplete, I would prefer to live.

I do not believe I would be alive today if Mommie had not gotten me to the hospital as quickly as she did and if I had not had the best of medical care, including the service of a pneumonia specialist. I am just as certain that I would not be alive if God had not seen fit to respond to the petitions of the loved ones and friends, some of whom had a continuous chain of prayer for twenty-four hours when I was at the worst stage of my illness. In other words, God stepped in in an unusual way and brought me through.

INTRODUCTORY QUESTIONS

I have suggested that God seldom, if ever, sends suffering or sorrow in some miraculous way. Rather, most of the time he would have to work a miracle to keep the suffering or sorrow from coming. What about the other side: Do you believe that God ever prevents or relieves suffering in a miraculous way?

What about the two examples of "healing" at the beginning of this chapter? Have you or a loved one had an experience similar to either of them? Do you believe it is possible that my experience was as much a miracle as Dr. Harris's? Which type of experience is most common? I have personally known very few who have had an experience comparable to that of Dr. Harris. In contrast, I have known many who, rightly or wrongly, have felt that God intervened in some miraculous way and pulled them through a serious illness.

Possibly, at least in a preliminary way, we should ask and answer the question, What is meant by a miracle? The dictionary definition is: "An event or action that apparently contradicts known scientific laws and is hence thought to be due to supernatural causes, especially to an act of God."

THE CREATOR AND THE CREATED

Are the miracles of God contrary to scientific laws or to the basic laws of life, or only apparently so? Another way of asking the same question: Are the miracles of God contrary to nature or simply beyond and above our knowledge of nature? We can correctly say that above and beyond any scientific laws is the law of God's own nature. One fundamental law is that the Creator is greater than what he has created. It may be that most of God's creative work is done through and in harmony with the basic laws of life, but as the Creator he can, and seemingly does at times, set aside or abrogate one or more of those basic laws. Any time the latter occurs, we can be sure that God sets aside a lower law for a higher one.

It seems that one purpose of the miracles of Jesus

was to reveal the authority of the Creator over what he had created. For example, he, who revealed the Father, spoke and the winds obeyed their master's voice (Matt. 8:26). Furthermore, Jesus, through his miracles of healing, revealed the Father's attitude toward sinning, sorrowing, suffering humankind. By his miracles as well as by his attitude in general, Jesus revealed a loving, compassionate Father. It should be a source of encouragement to all who suffer to remember that Jesus performed miracles to relieve suffering rather than to send it.

The question still remains: Does God still reveal his authority over that which he has created by performing miracles to relieve suffering and sorrow? It seems evident that striking miracles of healing are more rare in our day than they were in the days of Jesus and the early church. At least we do not often hear of miracles comparable to some performed by Jesus. He opened the eyes of the blind (Matt. 9:27–31; Mark 8:22–26), even of one born blind (John 9:1 ff.). He also healed a paralytic (Matt. (9:1–8), restored a withered hand (Luke 6:6–11), and healed those stricken with leprosy (Mark 1:40–45; Luke 17:11–19). On at least three occasions he raised the dead back to life (Matt. 9:18–19, 23–26; Luke 7:11–15; John 11:1–54).

It may be that such striking proof of the power of the Creator over the created is not needed today. We have the New Testament with its revelation and interpretation of God in Christ. We also have the witness of the Holy Spirit.

Another possible reason miracles are not needed as much now as formerly, at least in the United States, is that we have the resources of modern medical science. God evidently expects his children to use available resources. This may be why we hear more frequently of outstanding miracles on the mission fields where medical aids are less readily available. Whatever the reason, outstanding miracles of healing or relief do not occur as frequently now as in biblical days.

It seems clear that Jesus did not want to be sought out as a worker of miracles. He frequently requested the one who had been healed to keep silent about it. He evidently did not want his healing ministry to interfere with his more spiritual ministry to his disciples and to people in general. A study of the miracles of the early disciples, particularly Peter and Paul, reveals that the miraculous played a decidedly secondary role in their total ministry.

Prayer and the Physician

When I began to recover from my serious illness, I began to ask some questions that I have continued to ask. How did God heal me? How did he bring me back from the brink of the grave? He did not touch my body in some striking way and heal me. I spent four weeks in the hospital; most of five days in an oxygen tent. I experienced lingering weakness and a period of convalescence that usually follow any serious illness.

However, I believe I would not be alive today if God had not seen fit to step in and make the laws of healing, which are his laws, operate more effectively than they otherwise would have. In other words, his presence energized the laws. This was done, and I am persuaded it is frequently done, by giving doctors and nurses added skill and in making medicines more effective.

Do you think it is possible that my healing was just as much a miracle of God as the experience of my doctor friend when he walked away from his wheelchair? You know what my answer would be. The only difference is the method God used to perform his miracle. I am also persuaded that most contemporary miracles are worked through the operation of the laws of life. Really, we might see that the more striking miracles are in harmony with those laws if we had the proper understanding of how the laws of life operate.

If God is an active factor in the relief of suffering and sorrow, then prayer plays a significant part, not only in healing, but in the relief of suffering in general. Do you believe as I do that most and possibly all of God's relief of suffering is in harmony with and expressive of the basic laws of life? If you do, then you will agree that the physician and medical science in general are important agents in God's miracles.

Prayer and the physician belong together. Both have a place in the relief of suffering in general and in the healing of the sick in particular. The wise man in one book of the Apocrypha said that "healing comes from the Most High" (Ecclesiasticus 38:2). His admonition was "My son, . . . pray to the Lord, and he will heal you" (v. 9). He added, however,

> And give the physician his place,
>   for the Lord created him;
>   let him not leave you, for there
>   is need of him.
> There is a time when success lies
>   in the hands of physicians,
>   for they too will pray to the
>   Lord
> that he should grant them success
>   in diagnosis
>   and in healing, for the sake of
>   preserving life.
>   (vv. 12–14)

[63]

Many Christian physicians recognize that they are partners with God in the work of healing. They believe that "the prayer of faith shall save the sick" (James 5:15), but they also believe that the anointing with oil referred to by James (5:14; cf. Luke 10:34) represents their part in the healing process. Oil was used for medical purposes in New Testament days as it is today in many parts of the world.

God's Greatest Miracles

I do not belittle at all the marvelous physical miracles that God sometimes performs. I believe that many people have been and are being healed by him.

I am persuaded, however, and have been for many years, that God's greatest miracles are inner and spiritual. Some of these may be related to the physical healing process. God may contribute to the healing by giving the individual a greater desire to get well and a deepened faith that God will work with him or her in the process. The human mind and spirit has a tremendous effect on the body.

A young man approached me with a crutch on each arm but walking quite well. He did not need to introduce himself. I remember where he sat in a class of mine when he was preparing for a two-year term of foreign missionary service. He was strong of body and big of heart.

I remember when the news came that he had broken his neck and was being flown back from Africa to a hospital in the States. I had visited him with a doctor friend in the intensive care unit of the hospital. His condition was so critical that few believed he could live.

I had also visited him briefly a time or two while he was taking physical therapy treatments. There was strength and deep determination when he said, "By the grace and goodness of God I am going to walk again."

That night when he approached me on his arm crutches I asked Larry Hughes, "What about your fiancee?"

He replied, "Oh, we are married."

He is now serving as a general field counselor for the Texas Rehabilitation Commission. Larry is a demonstration of what God *and* the human spirit can do—or would it be better to say that he is a demonstration of what God *through* the human spirit can do?

God has also worked another kind of miracle in Larry's life. While he says that being handicapped and dependent on others is "very frustrating and almost unbearable at times," he also says, "What I have gone through and face every day has made a better person of me and makes me more dependent on God and more conscious of my need to look beyond myself."

Similarly, Dr. Cliff Harris says that far greater than the relief of his physical suffering has been the change in his life-style. He concludes, "The expression of joy, peace, and praise to God for his wonderful mercy and grace are wonderful. It changes the atmosphere of our home and family—particularly in love, peace, and security. There is a stronger feeling that God is real, personal, and cares."

There may be occasions when God will not see fit to remove the cause of our suffering or relieve our burdens, but he may work a marvelous inner miracle in our lives. We may discover, as Paul did regarding his thorn in the flesh, that the grace of God is sufficient for everything that comes with life. We may find it difficult to do so, but we should ask our heavenly Father for the grace to say with Paul, "Most gladly therefore will I rather glory in my infirmities, that the power of Christ may rest upon me" (2 Cor. 12:9).

Jesus performed some marvelous physical miracles while he walked on the earth. Possibly as great as any was his raising of Lazarus from the dead. I believe, however, that Jesus performed as great a miracle when he changed Simon the cussing fisherman into Peter the preacher on Pentecost and the early leader of the Christian church.

God performed a great miracle when he brought me back to life from the shadow of death. It was a greater miracle when, as a sixteen-year-old lad, he brought me from death into life in Christ.

I am grateful that I have been conscious of his miraculous working power in the years since both of these experiences. His grace and power have enabled Mommie and me to go on at times when it seemed we were at the end of our strength. We also thank the Lord that he has continued to perform spiritual miracles in our lives. We do not claim to know a great deal about him and how he functions in the world. We have had enough experiences with him, however, that we have abiding faith that he will provide for our needs and ultimately will receive us unto himself. Thank God for his miracles of grace!

7. The Contributions
of Suffering

W. R. (*Bill*) *Estep was a teaching* colleague of mine. He and his wife, Edna, and their three daughters and one son were fellow church members. Some time after the other children, Martin came into their home.

They knew before long that something was wrong with him. When he was about eighteen months of age, his health problem was diagnosed as cystic fibrosis, a disease that affects the whole body, particularly the sweat and mucous glands. With the best of care, the doctors told them that he could live only a few years.

Martin, an unusually intelligent child, was conscious of the seriousness of his illness. One morning, as a five-year-old, after an unusually difficult night when he was very ill with pneumonia, he said to his mother, "I thought I was going to be with Jesus last night."

Once when he and his mother heard a man give his Christian testimony on television, Martin said, "I want to do that."

His mother asked, "You mean become a Christian?"

"Yes."

His daddy and mother have no doubt about his experience with the Lord. This was when he was about seven years of age. About three or four weeks before his death, as if thinking aloud, he remarked to his mother, "You know, I would like to go up there and see what heaven is like."

Martin's life was short—he died when he was seven years and four months old—but the impact of his life lingers. His influence was and still is felt by every member of the family, by many others who were touched by Martin, and still others who felt his influence in the lives of his parents and other members of the family.

For Martin, for Martin's parents, and for all of us, the supreme question is not, Why suffering? but,

What will we let God do for us and through us because of our suffering? We can be sure that God wants to use any suffering or sorrow for our good and for the good of those touched by our suffering. He wants to speak to others through our suffering. Really, for Martin, as is frequently true, the suffering was a two-way street. He suffered; his parents and other loved ones suffered because of and with him.

What God is able to do for us and through us because of suffering depends on us. Martin's daddy says that although Martin died when still a child and in spite of his very serious illness, he lived positively. He had a maturity to accept and to adjust to the inevitable. God can use that kind of life, young or old, to bless those who are touched by it. That quality of life manifests the works of God (see John 9:3).

CONTRIBUTIONS TO THE SUFFERER

Regardless of why suffering comes or whether or not relief is provided, it will never leave the sufferer the same. It is doubtful that any experiences will shape and mold our lives as much as times of real suffering. Such experiences, to use an expression of Mommie's, "will make us better or bitter."

Whatever the effect of suffering or sorrow in your life, will you not agree with C. S. Lewis that "God whispers to us in our pleasures, speaks in our conscience, but shouts in our pain; it is his megaphone to rouse a deaf world"?

What does God teach us through our sorrow and suffering? Think through the following, some of which are closely related. Also make your own list growing out of your experience and observation.

1. Suffering can help us understand that character is built by solving problems, by carrying burdens. Just as strong muscles develop through exercise and alert minds result from solving difficult problems, so character is strengthened by meeting the storms and stresses of life.

2. Suffering may also contribute to the development in the life of the sufferer of obedience toward God and a movement toward the perfection found in Christ (see Heb. 5:8; 2:10). We can never become perfect, complete, or mature as he was, but in fellowship with him in our suffering we can move in that direction.

3. Suffering can teach us to be patient, a character trait that many of us need.

4. Suffering may also help to develop in us a proper evaluation of the values of life. We will tend to see more clearly that material things are instru-

mental and temporary. Health, life, and things immaterial will tend to be valued more highly.

5. Suffering can deepen our sense of a need for God. Someone has said that "one of the shortest roads to God is that of personal need," and in many of us suffering creates that sense of need.

6. Many of God's children have experienced a deepened fellowship with him as a result of their suffering. Some of us may be able to say with Job after his trying experience: "I have heard of thee by the hearing of the ear: but now mine eye seeth thee" (Job 42:5). Through his experience of suffering and his search for an explanation, Job acquired a personal knowledge of God as superior to his previous knowledge as seeing is to hearing. So it may be with us.

7. Closely akin to a deepened fellowship with God is a developing capacity to wait for him. The Scriptures enjoin us to wait on the Lord and frequently describe the blessings that come to the waiting heart. For example, the psalmist said, "Wait on the Lord: be of good courage, and he shall strengthen thine heart: wait, I say, on the Lord" (Ps. 27:14; see also Ps. 62:5; Isa. 30:15; Lam. 3:25–26).

You have seen this sign in a shoe shop: "Repairs made while you wait." Spiritual repairs may be made while we quietly wait in the presence of the Lord. No source is more effective for the relief of the problems, burdens, and sorrows that frustrate and sometimes defeat us than for us to rest in the Lord and wait patiently for him (see Ps. 40:1).

8. Another contribution that I am persuaded God would make to the lives of many who suffer is for us to learn how to pray "nevertheless." A "nevertheless" in prayer is not really meaningful unless it comes from a heavily burdened heart that has sincerely prayed "if it be possible, let this cup pass from me" (see Matt. 26:39). In other words, "nevertheless" is not an excuse for superficial, half-hearted praying. Earnest prayer that ends with a "nevertheless" is the way to a peaceful heart for the sufferer and for those who suffer with him.

9. One other possible contribution of suffering to the sufferer is difficult to express. It seems that most of us are like the strings of a violin. When the strings lie on a table, no music comes from them. Attach them to a violin, and some dull sounds can be heard. But when a skilled musician tunes the violin by drawing the strings tighter and tighter, they are ready to fulfill their purpose. Our heart-strings need to be drawn tight to produce the best harmony for the Lord. Suffering tightens the strings. The sufferer still needs, however, the Mas-

ter Musician to play on the strings of his or her heart if life is to bring forth the most perfect harmony.

CONTRIBUTIONS THROUGH SUFFERING

Many seriously handicapped individuals such as Helen Keller and Fannie Crosby have been inspirations through the years. Some of you know, as I do, handicapped individuals not as famous as Helen Keller or Fannie Crosby but who are just as courageous. Sometimes there is an equally courageous companion who stands by to share and to inspire. Clara Langston definitely belongs in that group.

Perry, Clara's husband, has been in a wheelchair since his spinal cord was severed during World War II. He was a graduate of one of our leading state colleges and was a commissioned officer in the army. He says that when he fell on the battlefield in North Africa, Romans 8:28 came to his mind. According to the doctors, he was supposed to die. He was brought back to a hospital in the States. The girl he had dated for about three years went to visit him. Two or three months later they were engaged. Clara says that she married Perry with a full knowledge of his condition. Now, after approximately thirty years of married life, she says, "I went into this with my eyes open and have never regretted the decision."

Later, Perry felt the call into vocational religious service. He attended a seminary and received a master's and a doctor's degree in religious education. All this he accomplished from his wheelchair, with Clara at his side most of the time. For several years he has been an effective teacher in a church-related college.

Another example of courageous achievement in spite of handicaps is Ruth Landes Pitts. She came into the world with deformed limbs and with a total of only four fingers. I remember clearly the visit I had with her parents, the James Landeses, soon after her birth.

During the first four years of her life, spent mostly in hospitals, doctors artificially created a third finger on her right hand and straightened her left leg so she could be fitted with a brace. She testifies she never considered her limitations a handicap but a challenge. As a child she ran and played with other children. What they could do, she did and frequently did better than they. She learned to cook, sew, and type.

In spite of her handicap, Ruth became a skilled pianist. She received her college degree in music education and completed a Ph.D. in music at George Peabody College for Teachers.

Her husband, whom she met as a college undergraduate, is a college teacher. They have two grow-ing, healthy sons. They maintain a busy life in church and community.

Ruth holds numerous professional memberships and has received many honors. The most recent honor has been inclusion in *Who's Who among International Musicians*. A brief biographical sketch of her has been included in Dishman's *Ten Who Overcame* (Broadman, 1966) and Swor's *Neither Down nor Out* (Broadman, 1966).

Ruth's exhortation to the handicapped is as fol-lows: "People—especially people with physical im-pairments—should think of the assets they have rather than the things they do not have or possess. People must realize that their lives can be either use-less or very meaningful. It is not the handicap but the attitude that makes the difference" (Dishman, p. 95). I am sure that Ruth will agree that the atti-tude toward one's handicap can be and frequently is determined, to a considerable degree, by the attitude of family and friends. In other words, the James Landeses are due considerable credit for Ruth Landes Pitts.

It should not be forgotten that many individuals like our Tom Mc are so seriously handicapped that they can never achieve the success of Perry Langston or Ruth Landes Pitts. You may be such an individual, or you may have one in your home. The best you can do is accept what has come, adjust to it, and seek to live triumphantly with it. Your reaction to your handicap or to the presence of a handicapped member of your family can be used by the Lord to make you a blessing to all who touch your life. What may seem complete defeat can become, by the grace of God, a marvelous victory. There is open to all of us, regardless of how dark may be the shadows or how heavy the burdens, a wonderful experience of a deepened life of prayer for ourselves and for others.

Our suffering can also open doors into the lives of others when no other key would fit the lock. It can enable us to enter into the suffering of others. This will be true to the fullest, however, only of those who have made a satisfactory adjustment to their own suffering. Those who have learned how to carry their own burdens with the help of the Lord are the ones who can be used most effectively by the Lord to lighten the burdens of others.

Paul wrote to the Corinthians that God "comforteth us in all our tribulation, that we may be able to comfort them which are in any trouble, by ["with," RSV] the comfort wherewith we ourselves are comforted of God" (2 Cor. 1:4). We are stewards of the comfort we have received from God. The purpose of his comfort to us is that we, in turn, may comfort others.

Chester Swor, a friend of mine for many years, has to an unusual degree comforted others with the comfort he received from the Lord. He has been a cripple since he was a lad. His "trademark" through the years has been a built-up shoe on his left foot, to compensate for a short leg, and a cane to assist him as he walks. Through the years he has been an unusually effective speaker and writer, particularly for young people.

Chester's personal conclusion is that his physical lameness has been one of life's richest gifts to him. He says, "From the fellowship of suffering I developed a deep desire to help to alleviate suffering which problems of any kind so often bring into people's lives."

He summarizes what his lameness has done for him in the following words:

Physical lameness has brought to me resources of strength which, otherwise, I might have failed to possess. It has brought to me, as only personal suffering can, an understanding of other people who suffer in body, mind, or spirit; and with that understanding has come a warm desire to *help*.

For me, physical lameness has opened windows, unlocked doors, widened horizons, deepened understandings, heightened sympathies, sharpened powers, and enriched with spiritual victories. Thank God for lameness!

What a triumphant note in those last four words: "Thank God for lameness!" My guess is that Chester Swor could not have said that in his younger days. Such a spirit and attitude are the work of God's grace. They come only to those who know that no handicap, no problem, however serious, can separate them from the love of God.

I hesitate to do so, but let me share a personal experience. On more than one occasion I have been asked to speak on "Why Suffering?" or on "God and Human Suffering." I was asked on two different occasions to speak to the same group. The second time some of the parents told me they would like for me to meet their children who were in another room in the same building.

As is true of many of the handicapped, the children reached out for love and understanding. They gathered close around me. I had my right arm around a little mongoloid girl and my left arm around a seriously handicapped boy.

I believe I can honestly say that I would have

[79]

given one of those arms that night if I could have touched that mongoloid girl or that handicapped boy and healed them. I do not believe I would or could have felt that way if our Tom Mc had not been in our home for years. I am persuaded that as Mommie and I have lived with him it has given us the desire, the compassion, and to some degree the capacity to enter into the suffering of others.

We have a deepening concern for people, particularly for people who suffer or carry heavy burdens. This is one contribution that I believe God has made to our lives through our experience with Tom Mc.

8. The Promises of God and Suffering

Some years ago I was working on a writing assignment for some material for church young people. In preparation, I was reading from the Minor Prophets. Suddenly one verse almost jumped out of the page at me. I did not remember having read or seen it before. Since that day I have never forgotten it. Over and over in the intervening years it has been a source of encouragement and strength.

You have doubtlessly had similar experiences. The Scripture that suddenly became alive for you may have been a Scripture of challenge or of comfort. It would be interesting if a group of us could share some of our experiences along this line.

CONFIDENCE IN THE PROMISES

When burdens become heavy or suffering intense, our minds and hearts seem almost instinctively to turn to the familiar promises of God. Our confidence in those promises is grounded in faith in his goodness and greatness.

During my Christian pilgrimage I have questioned, if not actually doubted, practically every aspect of the Christian faith except two things. First, I have never doubted the experience I had as a sixteen-year-old when I opened my heart and life and let the resurrected Christ come in to live. Two days after that decision as I was on my way to church the thought came to me: "These two days with Jesus have meant more than all the rest of my life combined."

The other aspect of my Christian faith that I have never seriously doubted is the dependability of the promises of God. Actually, the experiences of life have deepened and strengthened my confidence in those promises. Some of them have been put to the test and have not been found wanting. Over and over again as I have talked with disturbed and frustrated individuals, I have suggested: "Learn to rest, to relax, to let go in the Lord. Trust his promises."

If we could have a sharing session, what would be some of God's promises that have been most meaningful to you? Why these particular ones? Are some of them related to a specifically crucial period of suffering and/or sorrow in your life?

GENERAL PROMISES

Before we consider some promises for the terminally ill and before I share a few of my favorite promises, let me quote a few of many great promises in the Scriptures.

God's promise to Moses was: "My presence shall go with thee, and I will give thee rest" (Exod. 33:14). Also, "As thy days, so shall thy strength be" (Deut. 33:25). He would make the same promises to us.

The Psalms are full of marvelous promises. Among them are:

"The Lord is my light and my salvation; whom shall I fear? the Lord is the strength of my life; of whom shall I be afraid?" (27:1)

"God is our refuge and strength, a very present help in trouble" (46:1).

[83]

"Call upon me in the day of trouble: I will deliver thee, and thou shalt glorify me" (50:15).

"Cast thy burden upon the Lord, and he shall sustain thee" (55:22).

"In the day of my trouble I will call upon thee: for thou wilt answer me" (86:7).

"He that dwelleth in the secret place of the most High shall abide under the shadow of the Almighty. I will say of the Lord, He is my refuge and my fortress: my God; in him will I trust" (91:1–2).

Then there are some great promises in Isaiah, the prince of the prophets:

"Fear thou not; for I am with thee: be not dismayed; for I am thy God: I will strengthen thee; yea, I will help thee; yea, I will uphold thee with the right hand of my righteousness" (41:10).

"Fear not: for I have redeemed thee, I have called thee by thy name; thou art mine. When thou passest through the waters, I will be with thee" (43:1–2).

"Surely he hath borne our griefs, and carried our sorrows" (53:4).

"As one whom his mother comforteth, so will I comfort you" (66:13).

As we would expect, there are some very familiar and encouraging promises in the New Testament, including the following from the Pauline Epistles:

"For I reckon that the sufferings of this present time are not worthy to be compared with the glory which shall be revealed in us" (Rom. 8:18).

"And the peace of God, which passeth all understanding, shall keep your hearts and minds through Christ Jesus" (Phil. 4:7).

"But my God shall supply all your need according to his riches in glory by Christ Jesus" (Phil. 4:19).

"I know whom I have believed, and am persuaded that he is able to keep that which I have committed unto him against that day" (2 Tim. 1:12).

TERMINAL PROMISES

Is yours a terminal illness? Or do you have a loved one who has a relatively short time to live? Are you or they in considerable pain? If so, more than likely your mind and heart tend to recall the great promises in the Scriptures concerning life after death and the release that comes through death.

Jesus' statements recorded in John 14 are among the favorites of many terminally ill. To the disciples he said, and to us he would say: "Let not your heart be troubled: . . . I go to prepare a place for you. And if I go and prepare a place for you, I will come again, and receive you unto myself; that where I am, there ye may be also" (vv. 1–3). He also promised: "I will not leave you comfortless" (v. 18). Again he said to them, and would say to us: "Peace I leave with you, my peace I give unto you" (v. 27). It is his peace. There follow his words of appeal and assurance: "Let not your heart be troubled, neither let it be afraid" (v. 27).

No wonder Paul closed his great chapter on the resurrection with a question, followed by a note of triumph. The question: "O death, where is thy sting? O grave, where is thy victory?" The note of triumph: "But thanks be to God, which giveth us the victory through our Lord Jesus Christ" (1 Cor. 15:55, 57).

When I came home from the hospital after the serious illness mentioned earlier, our younger son, four or five years of age at the time, asked many questions concerning heaven that we could not answer. Several times we said to him, "Eugene, we do not know much about heaven—where it is or what the conditions will be there. There is one thing, however, that we do know. We do know that Jesus will be there. And if he is there, that will be enough."

PERSONAL PROMISES

May I now share with you some of my favorite promises? In two or three cases I will spell out briefly some of the background that may help to explain why they are favorites. In one or two cases they are only portions of verses.

First, Deuteronomy 33:27: "Underneath are the everlasting arms." We can rest on and trust those arms. These words come to me most frequently when I am thirty to forty thousand feet up in the air in a jet plane. That does not mean that one may not go down one day with me on it. If it does, still there will be underneath the everlasting arms.

Psalm 23 has been a favorite of mine for a long time, as I am sure it has been of many of you. However, when I was so seriously ill, something happened that has made it more meaningful ever since. My pastor and Mommie were the only ones permitted to visit me during the most serious part of my illness. One day when our pastor started to leave, he took my hand in his through the oxygen tent. He gripped it firmly, bowed his head, and simply said, "The Lord is my shepherd." He said no more; he knew that I knew the remainder of the psalm. Particularly reassuring in times of intense suffering or great sorrow is verse 4: "Yea, though I walk through the valley of the shadow of death, I will fear no evil: for thou art with me; thy rod and thy staff they comfort me."

However heavy the burdens or dark the shadows may be, the Lord is our Shepherd. The Shepherd knows his sheep by name, and the sheep know their Shepherd's voice. As was and is the custom in the Middle East, the shepherd goes before his sheep and they follow him (John 10:3–4). Our Shepherd will not ask us to walk in a way that he has not walked before us or in a way he will not walk with us.

Then there is Jesus' invitation which has meant so much to many through the years. "Come unto me, all ye that labour and are heavy laden, and I will give you rest" (Matt. 11:28). There follows another invitation and another promise. The invitation: "Take my yoke upon you, and learn of me; for I am meek and lowly in heart." The promise: "And ye shall find rest unto your souls. For my yoke is easy, and my burden is light" (vv. 29–30). The yoke is made easy and the burden light by the sense of his presence with us and in us.

Another promise that we can rest on in times of sorrow and suffering is Romans 8:28: "We know that all things work together for good to them that love God, to them who are the called according to his purpose." You may prefer, as I do, the Revised Standard Version's translation of this verse: "We know that in everything God works for good with those who love him, who are called according to his purpose." All things do not automatically work for good; it is God who in everything works for good. Notice also that our cooperation is required—"with those who love him." We may not be able to understand how this verse can possibly be true, but if we will accept it by faith, we will find it a great source of strength when suffering is intense, sorrows deep, and burdens heavy.

One other verse has been a great source of strength and encouragement to me for a number of years. I doubt if most of you will recognize it at all. It is the verse that jumped out of the page at me when I was studying the Minor Prophets. "When

I fall, I shall arise," and particularly the last portion of the verse, "when I sit in darkness, the Lord shall be a light unto me" (Mic. 7:8). I felt that I was in darkness that day, but as I meditated on the verse, I felt the light that comes from the presence of God creep into my soul and dispel the darkness. It seems at times that the darker the night, the brighter is the light that comes from his presence.

Conclusion

I would like to close with a quotation, an illustration, and a prayer.

The quotation: Our son Eugene gave me a statement from Victor Hugo a few years ago that has meant a great deal to me. Maybe it will help you.

Have courage for the great sorrows of life, and patience for the small ones, and when you have laboriously accomplished your daily task, go to sleep in peace. God is awake.

Faith that those last three words are true is the secret to a peaceful heart in the midst of conditions that would disturb and to a victorious spirit in times of sorrow and suffering.

The illustration: I heard George W. Truett use

the following illustration when he conducted the funeral for a pastor friend of his. He said that a young mother had died and left a four-year-old son. The night following the mother's funeral the father was awakened by the crying of his orphaned son. In the dark the boy cried out, "Daddy, are you there?"

The father, who had thoughtfully pulled the boy's bed over close to his, answered: "Yes, son, I am here," and reached out his hand and laid it on the boy's body. The crying lad grasped it in both his hands. His weeping soon ceased, and he was asleep again secure in the sense of the presence of his father.

Dr. Truett suggested that it can be that way with us and our heavenly Father in the midst of our darkest hours of suffering and sorrow. We can be sure he will be there to touch our lives and to comfort us if we will respond to his presence.

The prayer: *

O God, help me to go to sleep thinking of your
    promises.
The eternal God is your dwelling place;
    and underneath are the everlasting arms.
Help me to feel tonight
    the clasp of the love that will never let me go.
When you pass through the waters I will be with
    you.
Help me to feel you closest
    when life is sorest.

I will never fail you nor forsake you.
Help me to be very sure that, whatever happens,
    I do not have to face it alone.
Even the darkness is not dark to thee.
Help me to know that the darkest night
    is light, if you are there.
Help me tonight to believe in these promises and to
    rest in them: through Jesus Christ my Lord.
AMEN

—William Barclay
Prayers for Help and Healing

* New York: Harper & Row, 1975. Used by permission.

Summary

*In a few concise, closely related state-*ments I want to summarize the general position concerning suffering suggested in the preceding pages.

1. All of life is governed by certain basic laws. This means that a cause-and-effect relationship operates in all of life, including the area of suffering and sorrow.

2. The basic laws of life are written into the nature of men and women by the God who created them and into the world in which they live.

3. Some of these laws are known; others, un-known.

4. The benefits for the observance and the penalties for the violation of these laws are not external to the laws but inherent in them. This means that the results of obedience and disobedience are natural and inevitable.

5. Most, if not all, suffering results from the operation of the basic laws of life.

6. God does not in some miraculous way send suffering. In most cases he would have to work a miracle to keep it from coming.

7. Because the basic laws of life are in harmony with our natures, it is wise for us to seek to discover and to live in harmony with those laws.

8. Since sin is a violation of any law of God, un-written as well as written, most, if not all, suffering is the result of sin.

9. Sin that causes suffering may be the sin of the sufferer, but it may also be the sin of someone else or of society and/or the institutions of society.

10. Since God is sovereign of the universe, suffering in some way must be within his will. It seems clear, however, that it is a phase of his permissive or circumstantial will and not his perfect or intentional will.

11. God the Creator is more powerful than that

which he has created. He sees fit, however, with rare exceptions, not to interfere with the laws of life. This gives us a dependable, predictable world in which to live.

12. It does seem that God, at times, steps in in unusual ways to relieve suffering. He may do this by setting aside some of the basic laws of life, but it seems that more frequently he works in harmony with and through those laws. He energizes them and makes them function more effectively than they would without his presence.

13. Far more important than, Why suffering? is, What will we let God do to us, for us, and through us because of suffering?

14. God wants to use the suffering and sorrow that come to us for our good, for the good of loved ones and others, and for his glory. What he can do for us and through us will depend on our reactions to our suffering and to him because of our suffering.

15. Regardless of why suffering comes to us or the nature of our suffering, we can sense the presence of our heavenly Father and can confidently rest on his promises.